Charles
Darwin

A Cherrytree Book

Designed and produced by
A S Publishing

First published 1988
by Cherrytree Press Ltd
a subsidiary of
The Chivers Company Ltd
Windsor Bridge Road
Bath, Avon BA2 3AX

Copyright © Cherrytree Press Ltd 1988

British Library Cataloguing in Publication Data
Clarke, Brenda
    Charles Darwin.—(Children of history).
    1. Darwin, Charles—Juvenile literature
    I. Title II. Hook, Christa III. Series
    575'.0092'4   QH31.D2

    ISBN 0-7451-5000-4

Printed in Italy
By New Interlitho, Milan

457/90

CHILDREN OF HISTORY

Charles Darwin

By Brenda Clarke · Illustrated by Christa Hook

CHERRYTREE BOOKS

Erasmus Darwin (1731-1802), grandfather of Charles, was a respected scientist and writer. He was invited to become physician to King George III but instead in 1784 he went to Staffordshire as a country doctor. He became wealthy, and so fat that a hole had to be cut in his dining table to accommodate his stomach. He was a great friend of Charles's other grandfather, Josiah Wedgwood.

The Darwin Family

On Sunday 12 February 1809 a second son was born to the Darwin family who lived near Shrewsbury, on the English border with Wales. They named the boy Charles Robert. Charles was to become a famous naturalist, one of the greatest scientists of all time.

The Darwins' home was called The Mount and it overlooked the River Severn. Here young Charles grew up, with his older brother Erasmus and sisters Marianne, Caroline and Susan Elizabeth. Emily Catherine, the little sister, was just a year younger than himself. The children's mother, Susannah, was often unwell and kept to her bed. Her poor health was a great worry to her husband Robert, who was a wealthy doctor. Charles was much in awe of his father, not least because of his size. Dr Darwin stood 1.9 metres tall and weighed over 150 kilograms. He was, Charles later claimed, the biggest man he ever saw.

Following in Grandfather's Footsteps

Both Charles's parents came from distinguished families. His mother was the daughter of Josiah Wedgwood, the famous pottery manufacturer. His father was the son of Erasmus Darwin, a respected scientist, inventor and writer. As he grew older, Charles felt that he had a lot in common with his grandfather Erasmus. Both were fascinated by the natural world, especially by the enormous variety of living things. Erasmus had written a book suggesting that this variety had come about as living things had changed or *evolved*. He also wrote a long poem about the work of the Swedish naturalist Linnaeus, who had divided up all the plants of the plant kingdom into different varieties, or *species*, and had given each species a name.

An Original Work

As a child Charles knew of his grandfather's books, and in time he read them, and the writings of other naturalists. As a young man, he went on a long voyage around the world and studied the plants and animals of different continents. Years later he wrote his own book *On the Origin of Species*. This book explained how plants and animals had evolved into their various species.

Darwin's ideas changed for ever the way people looked at the world, and at themselves, because he also explained how he thought human beings had evolved. His books caused great argument and bitterness at first, although most scientists saw at once the greatness of his work. Today, the ideas of Charles Darwin are generally accepted as explaining how living things come to be as they are.

Charles and Emily Catherine were the youngest of the Darwin family. They saw little of their mother, who was an invalid and seldom strong enough to leave the house. Their father and their elder sister Caroline looked after them.

A Strict Childhood

Dr Darwin liked his house to be run in a highly disciplined way, according to his own strict views. Nobody felt much at ease in his presence, although Charles greatly admired his father and spoke of him as 'the wisest man I knew'.

A Sister's Supervision

Because their mother was an invalid, the older girls played a large part in running the household and in looking after the younger children. In later years, Charles could remember little of his mother, who died when he was eight. But he never forgot how he had to steel himself before meeting his sister Caroline, wondering what she would find to tell him off about now! Caroline was the best scholar among the girls, so she took charge of her younger brother and gave him lessons.

Soldiers were often to be seen in Shrewsbury when Charles was small. Britain was at war with France until the battle of Waterloo in 1815. Young Charles and the other young Darwins loved to watch local soldiers drilling outside their home.

Charles often seemed to be the cause of trouble. Although he considered his sister kind and clever, Charles wondered when he grew up if she had not tried too hard to improve him! Whatever mischief happened at The Mount, Caroline was sure that Charles was to blame. The older he grew, the more the sparks would fly between them.

Charles's Waterloo

Among Charles's other early memories was one of soldiers drilling outside his home, as the children watched excitely from the window. It was 1815, and across the English Channel, the Duke of Wellington was preparing to lead his army against the French soldiers of Napoleon Bonaparte. The people of Britain feared that if Wellington lost the battle, Napoleon's army would invade their shores. The uniformed men of the local militia parading outside The Mount might be called upon to defend Shrewsbury if the French came! But instead of defeat for Wellington there was victory at the Battle of Waterloo, and six-year-old Charles long remembered the happy celebrations which took place in the nearby town.

The Importance of Kindness

Kindness, for which Charles remembered his sisters, was considered of the greatest importance in the Darwin family. Charles was brought up to be kind not only to people, but also to animals. Both the Darwin and Wedgwood families believed in the benefits which advances in science and technology would bring to all people, rich and poor. Josiah Wedgwood in particular had encouraged his children to have humanitarian ideals. Above all, he hated slavery and produced a special pottery plaque in support of the anti-slavery movement.

GRANDFATHER WEDGWOOD
Josiah Wedgwood (1730-95) made a fortune from pottery-making in Staffordshire. His daughter married Robert Darwin and became the mother of Charles. Mrs Darwin was proud of her family and told her son how Josiah had met Queen Charlotte, wife of George III. The queen had admired his cream-coloured dinner services (later called Queen's Ware). Charles added to this story, telling schoolfriends that his grandfather had been a close friend of the queen!

PAINFUL MEMORIES
One of Charles's earliest memories was of himself at the age of four sitting on Caroline's lap as she cut up an orange for him to eat. Suddenly a cow ran past the window, making Charles jump. The knife slipped and cut his hand. He was reminded of the event ever afterwards by the scar left behind.

The Young Collector

When not at his books, Charles loved nothing better than to be outside, in the gardens at The Mount or beyond in the woods and fields. All his life he enjoyed being outdoors: as a child, playing, running and chasing; as a young man, shooting, fishing, riding and hunting; and as he moved towards old age, taking long walks every day. From the first, he took special notice of all he saw going on around him.

When the Darwin children went out to play, it was Charles who came home with a pocketful of 'specimens': stones, leaves, insects, flowers – anything which had taken his fancy. The urge to collect was to him the most natural thing in the world. Remembering what his sisters had taught him about kindness, Charles preferred to collect only dead insects as specimens.

The Bedroom Museum

Charles also gathered collections of pebbles, minerals, seashells, coins, letter seals and franks (which were like today's postage stamps). Soon his bedroom looked like a small museum, because the young collector was thorough and methodical with his exhibits. When he brought home a new specimen he first tried to identify it. Then, if he wanted to keep it, he mounted it on a tray, labelled it carefully and put it away neatly into a box or drawer. All scientists have to learn to be careful and accurate. This skill seemed to come naturally to Charles.

Learning About Nature

On warm, summer days Charles enjoyed visiting a nearby quarry pool, where he fished for newts. He also helped in

ONLY ONE EGG
Once in his eagerness to enlarge his collection, Charles removed all the eggs from a bird's nest. His sisters told him off; he should take a single egg only and leave the rest to hatch. Charles made this his rule from then onwards. For the time these were unusual and enlightened views. Now we know better than to touch a nest at all!

the garden at The Mount, learning the names of the plants as he dug and weeded. Soon he could identify most of the garden flowers, and those of the fields and hedgerows. He knew how they grew, how they produced seeds, and how their seeds were carried by birds or on the wind to fresh land where they could sprout into new plants.

A Fruitful Imagination

One day Charles ran in from the garden in great excitement to tell the family he had discovered a hoard of stolen fruit. His father was puzzled and eventually Charles admitted that he had picked the fruit himself from a tree in the garden and hidden it for fun. Caroline was furious, but his father did not mind too much. Charles often told stories. It seemed to Dr Darwin that this showed the boy had imagination and that some day it might be put to good purpose.

Charles kept his specimens tidily in trays and drawers. He tried to find dead insects to mount, but found his own way to kill live insects painlessly, using a mixture made from laurel and oleander leaves. Although Charles knew that animals and plants all had Latin names, he made up his own 'biological' names for his specimens and used these even when he grew up. Some of his beetle collection can still be seen today, each insect neatly labelled in pen and ink.

The Young Schoolboy

As Charles grew more unruly at home, it was decided that he should go to school. In the spring of 1817 he started at the day school in Shrewsbury High Street. Charles did not do well at his lessons. But he enjoyed the company of other boys and found among them a new audience for his 'tall stories'.

During the summer of this first year at school, Mrs Darwin died. Charles was then eight and a half, and the following year he was sent to join his brother Erasmus at Shrewsbury Grammar School. Shrewsbury was a highly respected place of learning, run by a famous headmaster, Dr Samuel Butler. Although they lived nearby, both boys boarded at school during the week and came home to The Mount at weekends. Charles also made unofficial visits home during the evenings but, being a fast runner, always got back to school before locking-up time at night.

Charles was always more interested in studying wildlife than in learning Latin and Greek verse. His masters thought him a poor scholar, and a rather ordinary boy. His friends enjoyed his tall stories: he claimed to one that he owned a Roman coin (it was really just 100 years old) and to another that he could change the colour of flowers by watering them with a 'secret liquid'.

10

In the Garden Shed

Charles later felt that school did little to prepare him for his scientific work. He learned Latin and Greek, and some geography and ancient history, but there were no science lessons. Neither his father nor his headmaster were pleased with Charles's progress and matters were made worse when Dr Butler discovered what the Darwin brothers did at weekends.

Erasmus's particular hobby was chemistry, and he persuaded his father to let him use a garden toolshed as a laboratory. With Charles as assistant, Erasmus spent most of his spare time setting up experiments. When Dr Butler heard of this he told the boys not to waste their time 'playing with chemicals'.

Charles's brother Erasmus was a keen chemist. In their garden shed the boys made a collection of apparatus – jars, retorts and test tubes – and carried out simple chemistry experiments. Their headmaster rebuked them in front of the whole school for these activities, and this caused Charles to be nicknamed 'Gas' thereafter.

A Trip to the Sea

Although he enjoyed helping Erasmus with his experiments, Charles's real interest remained in natural history. He spent the school holidays out of doors whenever possible, away from the solemn quiet of the house. But time passed slowly, and he was overjoyed when in the summer of 1819 he was allowed to join a teacher and several other boys on a visit to the Welsh coast.

Charles had been with his family on bathing trips to the seaside before, but now he had three whole weeks without them, to do as he liked. He swam in the sea with the other boys and joined them in races along the seashore. When the tide was out, he fished in rockpools for crabs and watched tiny fish darting among the weeds.

ROCKS AND FOSSILS
Until the 18th century, most people thought the world was 6000 years old. This belief was based on the Bible story of the Creation. But scientists studying rocks (geologists) knew how quickly rocks were forming in their own day, and realised that the earth must be much older.

Finding fossils made it possible to date the age of the rocks in which they were embedded. Charles

enjoyed chipping away with his hammer, hoping to find the fossil of a sea creature, such as an ammonite like this one.

Puzzled by Fossils

Charles found plants and insects he had never seen in Shropshire. He also found fossils which he chipped out of the rocks with a geological hammer.

Charles liked to find out as much as he could about his specimens, but nobody could tell him much about his fossils. Men working in the quarry near his home told him tales of fossils they had found as they cut down deeply into the rock. Some were kept on display in their cottages. But Charles was not interested in fossils as ornaments. He knew they were the remains of long-dead sea creatures, hardened into stone. He wanted to know exactly how long they had been dead and if he could find the same animals alive today. Nobody seemed to know for sure.

Although he listened with pleasure to Emma's playing and singing, Charles was impatient to know how the grown-up guests had fared at their shooting. When he was old enough to join the huntsmen, Charles kept his hunting boots by his bed, so as to waste no time in the morning.

Visiting the Wedgwoods

Twenty miles away from The Mount lived the Wedgwood family. The Darwins got on well with their relatives, although visits between the families had been rare because of Mrs Darwin's illness. But they exchanged presents at birthdays and Christmas, gifts from the wealthy Wedgwoods being particularly generous.

When he was ten, Charles went with his father to call on his uncle Jos and aunt Bessie. The Wedgwoods lived in a country mansion called Maer Hall, six miles from their pottery factory at Etruria. It was an Elizabethan house set in woodland and heath, which had been landscaped by the famous country house gardener 'Capability' Brown. The small lake (or mere) from which the house got its name was the main feature of the garden. The Darwin children loved the spacious grounds where they could walk and ride, and the lake where they could fish, swim, or take out a boat. In winter they made slides and skated on the thick ice.

Cousin Emma

Most of all the young Darwins loved the free and easy atmosphere at Maer, so different from their own home which was dominated by Dr Darwin. Uncle Jos could be forbidding too, but also kindly. The four Wedgwood boys and four girls were all older than Charles. Three of the boys were away from home at the time of this first visit, but the girls all took to their young cousin at once. Charles thought he liked Emma best. Although ten months older than himself, she seemed younger because she was so small.

Maer opened up a new world for Charles. He visited the house several times during the next five years, and enjoyed the happy family evenings of music and conversation with Uncle Jos's interesting guests.

Puzzled by Fungi

In the summer of 1824 Charles spent two weeks at Maer with the Wedgwoods, and it was during this time that he and his uncle Jos got to know each other well. Uncle Jos had a large library and encouraged Charles to read all he could, especially books about nature. A favourite book was the *Natural History of Selborne*, by a clergyman named Gilbert White. Charles found its account of birds so fascinating that he wondered why all gentlemen did not want to become ornithologists.

The grounds of Maer were familiar territory to Charles. But he still found new varieties of insects, especially moths, and discovered a new interest in mosses, lichens and fungi. Fungi puzzled him, for they were different in so many ways from other plants. Perhaps they were not plants at all.

Cousin Emma sometimes joined Charles on his fishing expeditions. She persuaded him not to use live worms as bait. Charles had other interests in the creatures and later made a long study of earthworms and their effect on the soil.

Writing the Truth

Charles delighted not only in observing, but also in finding out how things worked. He might have told outrageous stories as a child, but he grew up to hold the highest regard for the truth. To get at the truth you had to discover how things were made and how they functioned. Uncle Jos encouraged Charles to make full notes of what he observed. He must learn to write clearly and accurately and improve his use of language. To this end he read the great works of English literature, especially Shakespeare and Milton.

Hunting, Shooting and Fishing

Now that he was 16, Charles was old enough to join in the adult pastimes of Maer. Uncle Jos was a keen and generous sportsman, entertaining shooting parties on his estate. He taught his nephew how to use a shotgun and Charles thoroughly enjoyed himself tramping through the woods and fields, showing off his newly acquired skill at bagging grouse and partridges.

Next Uncle Jos presented him with a fishing rod and showed him how to bait the hook and handle the line. When much older, Charles disliked blood sports, but as a young man he loved to be out with the hounds.

A Disgrace to the Family

Dr Darwin, cross at his son's continued lack of progress at school, did not appreciate these new interests. 'You care for nothing but shooting, dogs and rat-catching and you will be a disgrace to yourself and all your family,' he told Charles. During the Christmas holidays of 1824, his father told him that he was to leave school the following year. He would join his brother Erasmus at Edinburgh University and study to become a doctor.

17

The Young Student

In the 19th century, medical students learned about the workings of the human body by dissecting corpses. Charles found the experience so horrifying that he attended only one class. He also hated watching operations without anaesthetics. James Simpson, a fellow Edinburgh student, introduced the use of chloroform in 1847 to make patients unconscious while surgeons operated on them.

Although not yet 17, Charles started studying at Edinburgh University in October 1825. He found most of the lectures dull and was disappointed that those in botany and zoology taught him no more about plants and animals than he already knew. His brother Erasmus left the university in 1826 and Charles made new friends. One of them told him about the French naturalist Lamarck and his views on evolution. Charles remembered that he had read ideas very like those in his own grandfather's books.

Soon Charles was missing lectures. Instead of sitting in a stuffy lecture hall he went out in a boat with fishermen trawling for oysters and found many new marine specimens to add to his collection.

BURKE AND HARE
Living in Edinburgh while
Charles was a medical
student were William
Burke and William Hare.
The two men were body-
snatchers, who stole
corpses to sell to doctors
and students for dissection
in anatomy lessons. Soon
Burke and Hare took to
murder to keep up the
supply of bodies. They
came under suspicion after
killing their 16th victim
and Hare confessed.

A Promising Young Man

In the summer of 1826, Caroline suggested that Charles
should go with her on a riding tour of North Wales.
Surprisingly, Charles enjoyed the holiday. Caroline had
changed her mind about him and now thought her brother a
promising young man. Charles continued studying sea
creatures in Wales and later gave a talk to a learned society
about some strange creatures called sea mats.

By his second year at Edinburgh Charles knew that
medicine was not the career for him. He found his first
dissection class so awful that he refused to go to another.
Neither could he bear to watch operations performed
without anaesthetic.

His father learned how distasteful Charles found his
medical studies. Anxious that his son would do nothing but
idle his time away in sport, Dr Darwin suggested that he
might like to become a clergyman instead. Charles agreed.

In Edinburgh Darwin met a
man who had travelled with
the naturalist Charles
Waterton. This man now
earned his living stuffing
birds, and Charles paid him
for lessons in taxidermy.
He found his teacher 'very
pleasant and intelligent'.

Happy Days at Cambridge

The idea of becoming a country parson appealed to Charles. He would study theology, but first he had to relearn all the Greek he had forgotten since leaving school. A tutor was summoned to The Mount and by January 1828 Charles was ready to enter Cambridge University.

Beetle Mania

The years at Cambridge were among the happiest Charles had known. He enjoyed student life, and managed to do just enough work to pass his exams. In the marshy countryside (fens) round about he found rare beetles and butterflies. Beetle-collecting became his favourite pastime. In winter he employed a man to scrape moss from old trees and bring it back to him in a bag. Among the creatures captured in the damp spongy moss were several rare species of beetle. More rare insects were found in the rubbish which Charles collected from the bottom of barges carrying reeds cut from the fens. He was enormously pleased to see the words 'captured by C. Darwin' beside a picture of one of his specimens in a learned book.

Learned Friends

One of the university scholars Charles most admired was the botany professor, John Stevens Henslow. The two men often went out walking together, or made excursions into the countryside to look for plants or rocks and minerals. Charles became known as 'the man who walks with Henslow'. He learnt a great deal from his new friend.

In addition to his own botany classes, Henslow sent Charles to lectures on geology given by Professor Adam Sedgwick, and encouraged him to read the work of experts such as Alexander von Humboldt.

At Cambridge, Charles met John Stevens Henslow (1796-1861), the young professor of botany, and Adam Sedgwick (1785-1873), the geology professor. Both were also clergymen. Sedgwick (below) helped Darwin to understand the 'scientific method' of working, while Henslow (above) recommended Charles for the job of naturalist on the *Beagle*.

Charles sometimes took a hired assistant with him when beetle-hunting, and always inspected his finds carefully. One day, Charles had seen two rare beetles at once. He grabbed one in each hand and then saw yet another. To pounce on this, he popped a captured beetle into his mouth. It let out a hot fluid which so burnt his tongue that Charles had to spit it out, losing another of his prizes in the confusion.

ALEXANDER VON HUMBOLDT
Alexander von Humboldt (1769-1859) was a German geographer and naturalist who explored in South America and central Asia. His *Personal Narrative* of his South American travels greatly impressed Charles.

Humboldt studied tropical storms, volcanoes, the earth's magnetic field, the world's climates and temperatures, and the distribution of plants around the world. He was interested in the links between all life on earth, and began the study we now call ecology.

21

Sports and Pleasures

Christ's College, Cambridge, where Charles studied, had a sporting reputation which suited him perfectly. He joined a group of high-spirited students who went duck shooting in the Cambridgeshire fens and raced horses across country. In the evenings they held supper parties where the guests drank, sang and played cards. Sometimes at such a party, Charles showed off his shooting skill. He would ask a friend to wave a lighted candle in the air. Then, aiming his empty shotgun at the flame, he pulled the trigger and snuffed it out with a puff of air from the gun's barrel.

Charles also discovered a taste for art and music. He spent many hours looking at the pictures in the Fitzwilliam Museum and listening to the choristers in King's College Chapel. Sometimes he hired the choir to sing in his rooms.

Charles enjoyed student life at Cambridge. On summer days, he and his friends would take out a punt for a leisurely afternoon on the River Cam, admiring the gardens and fine buildings of the Cambridge colleges.

NATURAL SELECTION

In 1809, the French naturalist Jean-Baptiste Lamarck (1744-1829) published a theory of evolution. He claimed that changes in an animal's living conditions caused it to change its habits and its form.

For example, the giraffe needed a longer neck as it was forced to stretch higher and higher to feed on leaves in the tree tops. Having lengthened its neck, the giraffe passed this characteristic on to its descendants and in this way a new species was formed.

Darwin thought that a new species formed by means of 'natural selection', which favoured giraffes that *happened* to have longer necks. They would find more tree-top food and so more would survive to breed longer-necked offspring. In time short-necked giraffes would die out and long-necked giraffes form a new species.

A Surprise in Store

Having passed his final exams in theology, in 1831, Charles left Cambridge. At Professor Henslow's suggestion he began a study of geology, mapping the rock formations near Shrewsbury. Henslow also suggested that he join Professor Sedgwick on a geological tour of Wales.

At the end of their short tour, Charles went home, eager to visit Maer for the partridge shooting. But waiting at home was a letter from Henslow that altered his whole life.

CREATION AND EVOLUTION

Lamarck was tutor to the son of the Comte de Buffon (1707-88), who first suggested the idea of evolution.

Erasmus Darwin and Lamarck had their own ideas on how animals changed form. All these men had a fierce opponent in Baron Cuvier (1769-1832) who believed that animals remained as they had been created.

Cuvier found fossils of extinct animals, but claimed they had died out in catastrophes such as Noah's Flood. New animals had then been created in another form.

James Lyell (1798-1875), a British geologist, argued against Cuvier. He said the earth had been changed by the same forces that are changing it still (the weather, the sea, volcanoes and earthquakes), and not by great catastrophes. Darwin read Lyell's book *Principles of Geology* on his voyage round the world. If the earth had slowly changed, perhaps its animals had too.

The Young Voyager

The *Beagle* was a ten-gun, three-masted brig, 27 metres long and just 245 tonnes. With 74 people squeezed on board, there was little room to spare. Darwin shared a cabin (far right) with Captain FitzRoy, who hoped the naturalist would find evidence of Noah's Flood in his explorations, or other clues to prove the truth of the Bible story of Creation.

Charles arrived home on 29 August 1831 and read his letter from Professor Henslow. It offered him a job from the Admiralty as naturalist aboard HMS *Beagle*, which was sailing on a scientific expedition to South America.

Charles was eager to accept at once, but Dr Darwin thought it a wild scheme. He forbade it, unless his son could 'find any man of common sense who advises you to go'. The man of common sense was Uncle Jos Wedgwood. At Maer next day, before the partridge shoot, his uncle told Charles that the voyage was a splendid opportunity for any young man. He persuaded Dr Darwin to change his mind and Charles wrote to accept the post. Then he set off, first for Cambridge, to see Henslow, and thence for London.

In London, Charles met Captain Robert FitzRoy, commander of the *Beagle*, and made arrangements for the voyage. He returned home to say goodbye to his family, Emma especially. Then he joined the *Beagle* at Portsmouth and sailed from England on 27 December, expecting to be away for two years. In fact the voyage lasted almost five years, and it took Charles Darwin right round the world.

Life Aboard Ship

The *Beagle* was small and Charles had to share a cabin with Captain FitzRoy by day and Midshipman King at night. His sleeping space was so cramped that he had to take out a drawer from a locker to make room for his feet as he lay on his hammock. For the first few weeks he was violently seasick and could eat only raisins.

The ship first anchored at the Cape Verde Islands, off the west coast of Africa, and Charles saw a volcanic island for the first time.

When the ship set sail again, Charles made a net to tow behind it in the sea. In it he collected many thousands of tiny sea creatures to study. The sailors laughed and complained at the mess on deck. But Charles kept on collecting his specimens, dissecting them, and recording his observations. He sent many specimens back to England. Henslow told other scientists of Charles's discoveries and made him famous long before he came home.

Captain FitzRoy was a religious man who believed, as some people still do today, that the Bible story of Creation was literally true. He hoped that Charles would find evidence of Noah's Flood. Like many people at that time, he thought the Flood explained the presence of fossil sea creatures in the rocks.

A BUTTON FOR 'CIVILIZATION'
The *Beagle* carried three passengers: York Minster, Jemmy Button and Fuegia Basket. They came from the islands of Tierra del Fuego off Cape Horn, at the tip of South America. Captain FitzRoy had taken them from their cold, windswept land on an earlier voyage to England. Here they had been educated, met the king and become Christians. Now they were to return home to spread 'civilization' to their people. Instead they went back to their traditional ways as if they had known no other. This much upset the religious Captain FitzRoy. Jemmy Button (above) was so named because his parents sold him for the price of a few buttons.

Charles's hunting skills were useful to the crew. In his tow net he caught fish to eat, and ashore he shot game. In Africa the crew had sampled ostrich dumplings, now they had roasted puma and armadillo cooked in the shell. For one Christmas dinner they ate guanaco, a llama-like animal that Charles had shot.

Charles set off on a mule to explore the Andes mountains. At 2000 metres he saw a fossil pine forest. Above it, at about 3000 metres, he found fossil sea shells. How did they get to be so high above the sea? Charles had his own theory: In prehistoric times the trees had grown by the Atlantic shore. Then the land sank under the sea. The trees were buried in mud and gradually turned to stone. Later, movements in the earth had pushed them upwards as the mountains formed.

Hunting Fossils

Some three weeks later, and 2000 miles across the Atlantic Ocean, the *Beagle* reached Brazil, and Charles saw his first tropical forests. Then they sailed south towards the tip of South America, enabling Captain FitzRoy to map the coastline.

In Argentina, Charles went fossil-hunting. He found hundreds of fossil seashells and animal bones embedded in cliffs. On the beach below he piled high his finds: a *Glyptodon* (a giant armadillo), the head of a *Megatherium* (a giant sloth), a *Toxodon* (like a hippopotamus) and a *Mylodon* (a sort of elephant). All were now extinct, yet Charles had also seen living armadillos and sloths. Was it not likely that they were related to the ancient giants?

FitzRoy believed that the great Flood had destroyed all life on land. Then plants and animals were created anew, and smaller. Charles disagreed. He thought the land must have risen above the sea, and that life had continued in an unbroken chain.

By summer the expedition had reached Tierra del Fuego, where there were passengers to put ashore. Back on the pampas (plains) of Argentina, Charles rode and explored with the gauchos. These tough cowboys were amazed at his energy. He trekked miles on foot and horseback and climbed every mountain he could. Twice he saved the lives of his companions by his speed and his stamina.

Moving Mountains

In Chile Charles experienced an earthquake and noticed afterwards that the land level had risen almost a metre. He pointed this out to FitzRoy. Charles was sure that the great Andes mountain chain had arisen in similar but more violent earth movements. That was easy to work out. Another problem was more taxing. How, Charles puzzled, had species living on remote islands made their way there?

On September 7 1835 the *Beagle* reached the remote Galapagos Islands in the Pacific Ocean. Here the answer to Charles's questions was to be found.

York Minster, Fuegia Basket and Jemmy Button rejoined their people in Tierra del Fuego. Life was hard in these bleak islands off Cape Horn and Charles thought the Fuegians more like wild animals than human beings. He was told they were cannibals. When the *Beagle* called at the islands again on its way home, only Jemmy Button was still friendly. They had left him plump and well dressed. Now he was thin, dirty and almost naked, but he ate supper on the ship as politely as ever.

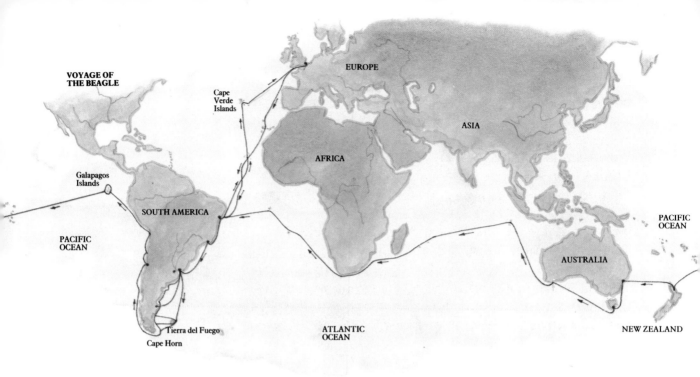

VOYAGE OF
THE BEAGLE

EUROPE

Cape
Verde
Islands

ASIA

AFRICA

Galapagos
Islands

SOUTH AMERICA

PACIFIC
OCEAN

PACIFIC
OCEAN

AUSTRALIA

Tierra del Fuego

NEW ZEALAND

Cape Horn

ATLANTIC
OCEAN

Tortoise Islands

The Galapagos Islands were discovered in 1535. Their name means 'giant tortoise' in Spanish. The *Beagle* landed on the Galapagos in September 1835, and FitzRoy left Darwin on James Island for the most important week of his life.

The islands were strange. In their dry, cactus-strewn valleys clambered giant tortoises, while dragon-like lizards called iguanas swarmed in thousands over the black volcanic rocks. All the birds were tame. Darwin found 26 species of birds on one island alone.

Back on the ship, Charles sorted out his specimens. Most of the species were unknown elsewhere in the world. And each island had its own different species. The giant tortoises of each island had different shells and different-shaped necks. The finches had different beaks.

The *Beagle*'s five-year voyage circled the earth. From the Galapagos Islands (below) the ship sailed to New Zealand and Australia.

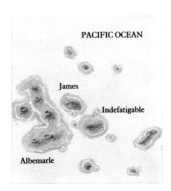

PACIFIC OCEAN

James

Indefatigable

Albemarle

28

Darwin did not grasp at once what all this meant. But he now knew that animal species did not remain the same for ever.

New Islands, New Species

From his observations on the islands, Darwin worked out their story. They had been pushed up from the sea by volcanic eruption. First there was no life on them. Then birds arrived, dropping seeds. More seeds were washed ashore and plants grew. Lizards and tortoises probably arrived on floating logs.

Each animal had to adjust to eating the food it found on the various islands. Animals which could not adapt died out. The creatures best able to adapt survived. Darwin called this 'natural selection'.

Over the generations, animals descended from a common ancestor changed their forms as they adapted to living on different islands. They became so different from each other that they could not inter-breed. They had formed new species.

On the Galapagos Islands live 13 species of finch, each with a different-shaped beak. Darwin realised that all the birds had a common ancestor which had flown there from the mainland. In time they had evolved different beaks, each suited to the foods they found on various islands. Studying the finches helped Darwin to form his 'natural selection' theory of evolution.

Darwin noticed that the giant tortoises of the Galapagos had different shell shapes and necks, according to which island they came from. People familiar with the islands could tell at a glance which tortoise lived on which island.

The Famous Scientist

After he arrived back in England, on 2 October 1836, Darwin began work on the specimens he had collected during the voyage. In 1839 he married his cousin Emma and went to live in Downe, Kent. Here he spent the rest of his life in study and writing, working out his theory of evolution by natural selection.

Survival of the Fittest

Although his friends knew of Charles's ideas, he did not publish them for 20 years. Then in 1858 he heard from another naturalist, Alfred Russel Wallace (1823-1913). Wallace had formed his own ideas on evolution and his notion of the 'survival of the fittest' was very like Darwin's view. A paper by both men was read to a learned society in July 1858 and the next year Darwin published his most famous book. It was called *On the Origin of Species by means of Natural Selection.*

The book caused a great stir, and made Darwin many enemies among people like FitzRoy who believed only in the Bible story of the world being created in a week.

The Evolution of Our Knowledge

In 1871 Darwin published *The Descent of Man*, saying that human beings were also the result of evolution. They and the other primates, the great apes, were descended from a common ancestor. People found it hard to accept these ideas. They changed the whole course of human knowledge. But scientists knew their truth. Darwin studied and wrote for the rest of his life. He died on 19 April 1882 and, as an honour to perhaps the greatest naturalist of all time, was buried in Westminster Abbey.

Charles and Emma Darwin lived at Down House in Kent. Here they brought up their ten children and Charles worked on his books.

Important Events in Darwin's Life

1809 Born near Shrewsbury, England, on 12 February.
1817 Mother dies (July). Starts school at Mr Case's school in Shrewsbury.
1818 Moves to Shrewsbury Grammar School.
1819 Makes his first visit to Wedgwoods at Maer Hall.
1825 Leaves school and goes to study medicine at Edinburgh.
1828 Admitted to Cambridge, to study theology at Christ's College.
1831 Graduates from Cambridge and invited to join the *Beagle* voyage as a naturalist. Leaves England on 27 December.
1832 Visits Cape Verde Islands, Brazil and Tierra del Fuego.
1833 In Argentina, exploring the pampas.
1834 In the Andes Mountains of Chile.
1835 Witnesses effects of earthquake in Chile (February). *Beagle* reaches the Galapagos Islands (September). Journey home includes stops at Tahiti (November 1835), New Zealand (December 1835), Australia (January 1836).
1836 After one last visit to South America, *Beagle* returns to England, and lands at Falmouth on 2 October.
1839 Marries Emma Wedgwood, 29 January, and for three years lives in Upper Gower Street, London.
1842 Moves to Down House in Downe, Kent. Publishes book on coral reef formation and works on outline of 'species theory'.
1845 Journal of *Beagle* voyage is published.
1856 Starts to write full account of species theory.
1858 Learns that Alfred Russel Wallace has also come to the same conclusions about evolution. Darwin's and Wallace's theories on the subject are read before the Linnaean Society in London.
1859 Publication of *On the Origin of Species*.
1871 Publication of *Descent of Man*.
1882 Dies at Down House (19 April).

Darwin lived at Down House for 40 years. He wrote about coral reefs, volcanic islands and the geology of South America. He studied all sorts of plants and animals, such as barnacles, earthworms, pigeons, orchids and insect-eating plants. He was often unwell, probably as a result of insect bites in South America. But even as an old man he walked every day in his garden, still ready to marvel at the amazing variety in all the living things around him.

Index

Withdrawal